Fantastic Book of Logic Puzzles

By Muriel Mandell
Illustrated by
Elise Chanowitz

 Sterling Publishing Co., Inc.   New York

Library of Congress Cataloging-in-Publication Data
Mandell, Muriel.
  Fantastic book of logic puzzles.

  Includes index.
  Summary: A collection of seventy illustrated logic
puzzles set in fantastic locales such as outer space or
mythical kingdoms, with explanations of the logical
reasoning needed to solve them. Includes charts, grids,
diagrams, and a section of clues to consult before
resorting to the answer section.
  1. Puzzles—Juvenile literature. 2. Logic—
Juvenile literature. [1. Puzzles. 2. Logic]
I. Chanowitz, Elise, ill. II. Title.
GV1493.M25 1986   793.73   86-5980
ISBN 0-8069-4754-3
ISBN 0-8069-4756-X (pbk.)
ISBN 0-8069-4755-1 (lib. bdg.)

Published by Sterling Publishing Co., Inc.
387 Park Avenue South, New York, N.Y. 10016
Distributed in Canada by Sterling Publishing
℅ Canadian Manda Group, P.O. Box 920, Station U
Toronto, Ontario, Canada M8Z 5P9
Distributed in Great Britain and Europe by Cassell PLC
Artillery House, Artillery Row, London SW1P 1RT, England
Distributed in Australia by Capricorn Ltd.
P.O. Box 665, Lane Cove, NSW 2066
Manufactured in the United States of America

For Horace

ACKNOWLEDGMENTS

I would like to acknowledge my debt to Irving M. Copi's *Introduction to Logic*, to master puzzlemaker Henry Ernest Dudeney, to Martin Gardner, and to Fred Schuh. The following looked over the manuscript and offered suggestions: mathematician and puzzle-enthusiast Dr. David Greenwald; Dr. Arnold Scheiman of Park West High School; Dr. Ira Ewen, Director of Thinking Skills of the New York City Public Schools; and Edith Novod, Arline Beitler, Stanley Beitler, Jonathan Mandell, and Horace Mandell. The book would never have been written without the encouragement and editorial guidance of my editor at Sterling, Sheila Barry.

And thanks too to the many readers who, since the book's publication, have written with suggestions and alternate solutions. Some have been incorporated in this revised edition.

Contents

Before You Begin

Puzzles are a time-honored fun-filled way of learning to reason logically, to develop thinking skills. They serve the same function for the mind as exercise does for the body. And they've been doing it for centuries.

Puzzles have provided intellectual pleasure for the thinkers of every age, from the early Egyptians, the legendary Oriental philosophers, the ancient Greeks, and such renowned medieval scholars as Alcuin and Rabbi Ben Ezra.

But logic puzzles are no mere entertainment. Many practical disciplines, including geometry, developed—at least in part—from the concepts and ideas in these mathematical games. The highly useful theory of probability, on which so much of our modern life is based, supposedly stemmed from an attempt by the 17th century mathematician Pascal to solve a gambling dispute! (This is the self-same Pascal, by the way, who at 19 invented one of the early calculating machines.) And the formulas in the "Wizards of Odds" are used by handicappers and economists alike.

You'll find examples of many popular types of logic puzzles in this book. It's not necessary to start with any particular chapter, but it is a good idea to concentrate on one chapter at a time and complete most of the puzzles in it—preferably in order—before you go on to the next.

Each chapter starts with the simplest puzzles of a particular type, so that you build up your understanding and skills step by step. If you get stuck, you'll find help in the "Clues" section of the book, which starts on page 83. Sometimes the hint will point out a tricky bit of language, sometimes it will reveal the particular approach to take. Occasionally, it will give a simple formula, the mathematical shorthand for the logical thinking involved.

But with these logic puzzles, getting the correct answer isn't nearly as important as figuring out *how* to find it. Therefore, for each puzzle, no matter how easy or difficult it is, a detailed explanation is provided at the back of the book. If you come up with different methods of solving any of the puzzles—techniques you think are better, easier or quicker than the methods described in the answer section—do send them on so that we can share them with other puzzles fans in subsequent editions.

Why are all the puzzles set in "fantastic" situations? Strictly for fun. Because imaginative and humorous settings stimulate the imagination and make it more interesting to master the verbal and mathematical skills needed. What's more, they are much more fun to write!

So—off to interplanetary space, to mythic kingdoms, to Arabian nights and to medieval magic. Have a mind-bending trip!

Would Martians Lie?

s that alien telling the truth or lying? How can we tell?

In real life, when faced with someone who may or may not be lying, we are often influenced by body language, by a look in the eye, by a stray word, by our emotions or by our prejudices. But in these truth puzzles, we have to rely on logic alone!

1. The Martian Rub

After his spaceship landed on Mars, astronaut Jonathan Mark disembarked and approached the first Martian he saw.

"Am I headed for the geological dig?" he asked.

The Martian rubbed his stomach.

Mark knew that Martians could understand some Earth-talk, but were not able to speak it. And astronaut Mark, like so many Earthlings, could neither speak nor understand Martian gestures. He didn't know whether rubbing the stomach meant yes or no. But by asking one additional question, Mark was able to find out.

What was that question?

2. Stone Stew

After astronaut Mark got to the dig, he collected rock specimens to take back to the Earth scientists. He packed the rocks into three sacks: one for igneous rocks, one for sedimentary and one for metamorphic. But, rushing to return to the aircraft before his portable oxygen ran out, he mislabelled all the sacks.

How many rocks did he have to take out of how many sacks in order to find out what was in each one?

Clues on page 84.
Answers on page 94.

3. Friend or Foe?

Among the inhabitants of Mars were various kinds of creatures. One type was friendly to visitors from Earth and always told the truth. Another was hostile and always lied to Earthlings. But the astronauts couldn't tell the difference between them.

"Are you a truth-teller?" astronaut John Armstrong asked a striped Martian he met on the way to the dig.

"He'll say, 'Yes,' " commented a spotted Martian who was nearby. "But he'll be lying."

Who was the truth-teller, the striped Martian or the spotted one?

4. How Many Liars?

Molly Ride, pilot of the spacecraft, knew that some Martians were truth-tellers and some were not. So when she came face to face with three of them, she asked, "Are you truth-tellers?"

The finned Martian answered her by rubbing his stomach. His friend, a tall Martian with feathered ears, told her that the finned Martian had said he was a truth-teller. However, the other Martian, who had horns, said that the finned Martian was lying.

How many of these Martians were liars?

Clues on page 84.
Answers on page 94.

5. The Search for Doman

This was astronaut José Perez's fourth visit to Mars and he had learned to speak Martian. He wanted to find his Martian friend Doman, but in order to locate him he had to know what group Doman belonged to. The three groups in the area were: Uti, Yomi, and Grundi.

The Uti always told the truth.

The Yomi always lied.

The Grundi sometimes told the truth but sometimes lied.

Perez needed information. Three Martians, Aken, Bal and Cwos, each of whom belonged to a different group, agreed to help him. He asked each one of them two questions: What group do you belong to? What group does Doman belong to?

1. Aken said:
   I am not a Uti.
   Doman is a Yomi.
2. Bal said:
   I am not a Yomi.
   Doman is a Grundi.
3. Cwos said:
   I am not a Grundi.
   Doman is a Uti.

What group does Doman belong to?

Clue on page 84.
Answer on page 95.

6. Martian Mystery

There was trouble from the Grundi. One of them damaged the spaceship by hurling a rock at it. The astronauts couldn't figure out what the Grundi had to gain by their hostile act. Was it just vandalism, done out of sheer spite? Or perhaps not everyone on Mars was happy to see the Earthlings return.

The Martian police chief brought in five Grundi for questioning. Like all Grundi, they sometimes told the truth and sometimes lied. The suspects each made three statements, two of which were true and one of which was false. And the guilty one was revealed.

1. Zum said:
   I am innocent.
   I have never used a rock to destroy anything.
   Tset did it.
2. Uk said:
   I did not do the damage.
   The Earthman's vehicle is on Grundi space.
   Yan is not my friend.
3. Pala said:
   I am innocent.
   I never saw Yan before.
   Tset is guilty.
4. Tset said:
   I did not throw the rock.
   Yan did it.
   Zum did not tell the truth when he said I did it.
5. Yan said:
   I am innocent.
   Uk is guilty.
   Pala and I are old friends.

Who was the culprit?

Clue on page 84.
Answer on page 95.

Planetary Crossings

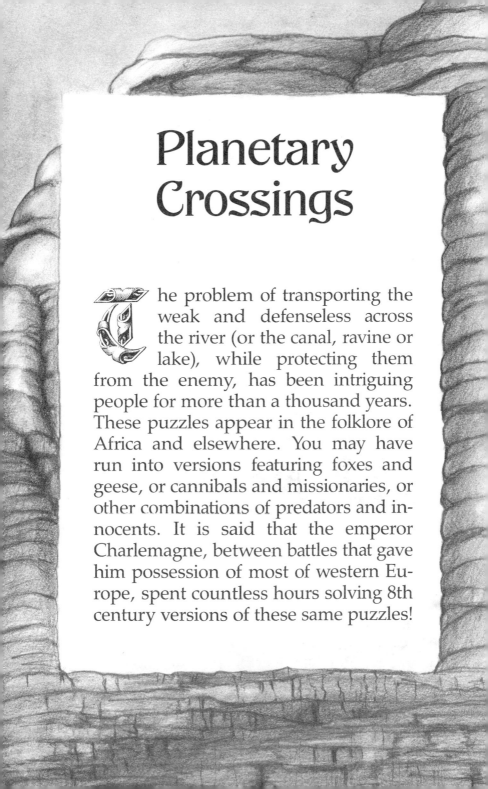

The problem of transporting the weak and defenseless across the river (or the canal, ravine or lake), while protecting them from the enemy, has been intriguing people for more than a thousand years. These puzzles appear in the folklore of Africa and elsewhere. You may have run into versions featuring foxes and geese, or cannibals and missionaries, or other combinations of predators and innocents. It is said that the emperor Charlemagne, between battles that gave him possession of most of western Europe, spent countless hours solving 8th century versions of these same puzzles!

7. Tsientsien Don't Eat

Jonathan Mark gathered three specimens of Martian plant and animal life to bring back to Earth: a garble, a farfel and a tsientsien. But Mark was worried. His vehicle for local travel was not big enough to hold more than himself and one specimen. Mark knew that garbles will eat farfels if given half a chance, and farfels will eat tsientsien. Garbles, however, don't eat tsientsien, and tsientsien don't eat. All the other astronauts were away from the ship. How could Mark transport the garble, the farfel and the tsientsien one at a time so that they would all be safe?

8. The Gravity on Mars

Two Martians and two Earthlings traveling together came to a canal. As a result of the gravity on Mars, the Earthlings each weighed 100 pounds and the Martians fifty pounds. The watercraft would hold no more than 100 pounds. How did they all cross the canal?

Clues on page 84.
Answers on page 96.

9. Rockfall

Harassed during important experiments, three Earthlings were taking three law-breaking Grundi to the authorities. Suddenly they heard the thunderous roar of a rockfall, and they knew they were facing sure death unless they crossed to the other side of the canal. The portable watercraft they carried with them would hold only two passengers, regardless of weight. At no time could there be more Grundi on either side of the water than Earthlings or the Grundi would overpower the Earthlings and steal the pulleys and ropes needed to travel the hazardous area. How could they all cross the water safely?

10. Fins and Feathers

Hostile members of the Uti, Grundi and Yomi groups were travelling to a conference. There were two members from each group, one finned and one feathered. The finned Martian was much stronger, and had to protect her feathered friend. Never could a feathered Martian be left alone with a finned Martian of another group. The only time a feathered Martian was safe with the finned Martian of another group was when the feathered Martian of that group was also present.

The trip was quiet until they came to a deep ravine. The only way to cross it was by swinging across on a rope. But the rope was only strong enough to hold two of them. And it wasn't heavy enough for them to swing it back over the ravine without someone to weigh it down. How did they all cross the ravine?

Clues on page 84.
Answers on pages 96–97.

Martian Mischief

When you think of a logic puzzle, the type of brain-teaser in this chapter probably comes to mind. Here you receive fragmentary information about a situation involving an assortment of people, places and things. By putting the information together and eliminating the impossible, you eventually form a picture of who is related to whom, or who does what, when.

If these puzzles appeal to you, you're in good company. Mathematician Charles Dodgson who, as Lewis Carroll, wrote *Alice's Adventures in Wonderland*, was also entranced with puzzles like these and invented many of them.

11. Flying Teams

Martians don't need to develop airplanes as a means of moving through the air. Most feathered Martians can fly easily. Every few lunars, feathered Martians from the various groups participate in a tournament to determine which are the best fliers of the planet.

This lunar, teams of two feathered Martians from three groups are competing:

1. One team is from the Uti, one from the Grundi, and one from the Yomi.
2. Each team is made up of one female and one male.
3. The female participants are Xera, Wora, and Teta.
4. The males are called Vel, Pyi, and Rir.
5. Despite her daring feats in the air, Teta had never been away from home before the contest.
6. Xera and Rir had never met before the tournament.
7. Xera will be visiting Pyi's group when the Yomi go on a special excursion to that part of the planet.
8. Pyi admires Teta's colorful feathers, as well as her ability to soar, and once watched her and her teammate in the territory of the Grundi.

If the winners are members of the Uti group, what are the names of the best fliers?

Clue on page 85.
Answer on pages 97–98.

12. Spaceship Crew

Kim Jones, Jan Robinson and Pat Smith are the officers of the spaceship. They serve as the craft's pilot, engineer and biochemist, though not necessarily in that order. Because they have difficulty with Martian names, they nickname the three Martians who work with them Jones, Smith and Robinson.

1. Robinson is a Yomi.
2. Jones doesn't speak any language other than Martian.
3. All Martian linguists are Uti.
4. The Martian who serves as interpreter respects the Martian whose name is the same as the biochemist's.
5. The Martian whose name is the same as the biochemist is a Grundi.
6. Jan Robinson beat the engineer at chess.

Who is the pilot?

Clue on page 85.
Answer on pages 98–99.

13. A Flock of Martians

Four Martians from different groups, the Uti, Grundi, Yomi and Rafi, gathered for an intraplanetary conference to discuss the problem of the visiting Earthlings. As was appropriate for diplomatic envoys, all were beautifully feathered in different colors, one red, one green, one blue and the fourth brown. Their names were Aken, Bal, Mun and Wora.

1. Before the meeting, the Uti had a pleasant breakfast with Mun.
2. After debating with the Martians in the blue and the brown feathers, Bal and the Yomi were so angry that they tore a wingful of feathers out of them before they were stopped.
3. Wora and the Rafi, however, agreed with the diplomat with brown feathers, though they disagreed with the red-feathered Grundi.

Who is the blue-feathered diplomat and to what group docs he or she belong?

Clue on page 86.
Answer on pages 100–103.

14. Aken's Friend

On the day before the spacecraft was to return to Earth, the Martians held a dinner party for the crew. In all there were eight at the table: Aken, Bal, Mun, Mark, Wora, Jones, Rider and Smith.

    a. One was a history buff.
    b. One was a whiz at math.
    c. One was very tall.
    d. One was Aken's friend.
    e. One had yellow feathers.
    f. One was a pilot.
    g. One was a rock collector.
    h. One spoke a number of languages.

1. The person who was Aken's friend sat directly opposite Mark, the rock collector.
2. Wora sat between the math whiz and Aken's friend.
3. The tall one sat opposite Wora, with Aken to her left.
4. Smith, who had no real friends among the group, sat to the right of Mun who towered over the rest of the group.
5. The one who had yellow feathers sat opposite Bal, between Mun and the one who spoke a number of languages.
6. Jones was to the right of the rock collector and opposite the pilot who was next to Rider.

Who was Aken's friend?

Clue on page 86.
Answer on pages 103–105.

Matching Wits

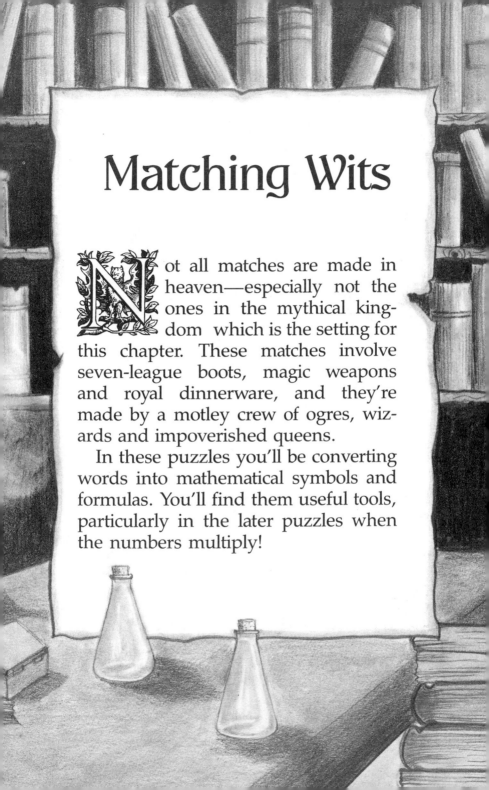

Not all matches are made in heaven—especially not the ones in the mythical kingdom which is the setting for this chapter. These matches involve seven-league boots, magic weapons and royal dinnerware, and they're made by a motley crew of ogres, wizards and impoverished queens.

In these puzzles you'll be converting words into mathematical symbols and formulas. You'll find them useful tools, particularly in the later puzzles when the numbers multiply!

15. In the Dark

Planning to roam the countryside and prey upon its defenseless people, the ogre reached into his dark closet. There he had stored four six-league boots and eight seven-league boots. How many boots did he have to pull out of the closet to make sure he had a pair that matched?

16. Sword Play

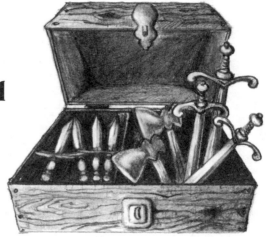

The local king, determined to defend his kingdom from that wicked ogre, sent his two eldest sons to the court swordsmith.

The swordsmith kept a supply of special ogre-fighters (four daggers, three swords and two axes) locked in a chest. The two princes insisted on having the same kind of weapon.

How many weapons did the swordsmith have to take out of the chest to be sure he could meet the demands of the princes?

Clues on page 87.
Answers on pages 105–106.

17. Royal Dinner

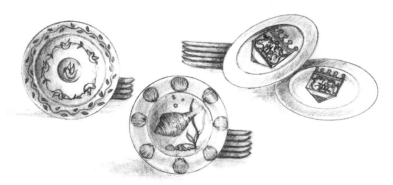

To enlist the help of the other kingdoms, the king talked to the queen about inviting neighboring royalty to dinner. This put the queen into a royal snit. Theirs was not a very wealthy kingdom and the royal dinnerware was in a disgraceful condition. Apart from ordinary dishes for everyday use, all that the royal pantry contained were a few dinner plates of three different dinner patterns:

1. five silver ones with birds
2. six crystal with seashells
3. seven gold with the royal crest

They were all stored in disarray on a very dark top shelf of the royal pantry. Only those would be suitable for entertaining other royalty.

If the queen didn't want to climb up to the top shelf twice, how many dinner plates would she have to take down to be sure she had matching dinner plates for herself, her royal spouse, and for the neighboring king and queen?

Clue on page 87.
Answer on page 106.

18. Anti-Ogre Potions

The king had his doubts about his sons' fighting skills, and so he sent his two eldest to the court magician for potions to help fight the ogre.

The magician kept his magic hidden, mindful of the danger of his potent potion falling into the wrong hands. In a secret but inconvenient compartment in his laboratory, he hoarded:

1. four ogre-fighters
2. three dragon-destroyers
3. two evil wizard-vanquishers

How many potions did he have to reach for in order to make sure that he could give an ogre-fighter to each of the king's two sons?

Clue on page 87.
Answer on pages 106–107.

19. Seven-League Boots

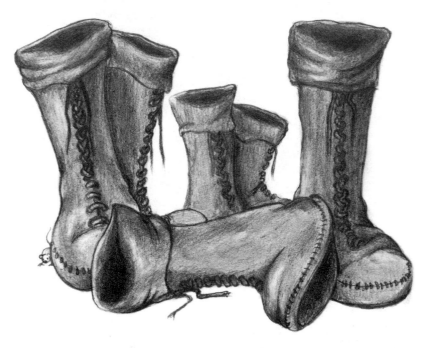

Meanwhile, back at the castle, the ogre found that the boots he had picked at random from his dark storeroom were all six-league boots. He threw them back. He needed seven-league boots so that he could cover more territory.

If in that dark storeroom he had four six-league boots and eight seven-league boots, how many boots did he have to pull out to make sure he had a pair of *seven-league* boots?

Clue on page 87.
Answer on page 107.

In the Ogre's Dungeon

 ike the truth puzzles in "Would Martians Lie?" and the elimination puzzles in "Martian Mischief," the brainteasers in this chapter are classic problems in logic. After the first few puzzles that get you started, they all involve "if" statements. The conclusion depends on the "if" part being true.

Once you learn how to think them through, you may find these puzzles more entertaining than almost any other kind. If you like them, go on to the chapter called "Genie Devilment," in which you have to deal with *several* conditional statements—several "if's"— in a single puzzle. Those are even more challenging.

20. In the Forest

The king's only children, Abel, Benjamin and Paula, went into the forest with their friend, the elderly Sir Kay. They wanted to try their skill with their bows and arrows. Each of them started with same number of arrows. When all the arrows had been shot, it was discovered that:

1. Sir Kay brought down more game than Princess Paula.
2. Prince Benjamin captured more than Sir Kay.
3. Princess Paula's arrows went truer than Prince Abel's.

Who was the best marksman that day?

Clue on page 87.
Answer on page 107.

21. Captured!

Happy at the hunt, the king's children became care-less and less watchful than usual. A passing ogre easily captured them and Sir Kay and took them back to his dungeon. He placed them in four cells in a row.

The cell in which Prince Abel was held prisoner was next to Prince Benjamin's. But Prince Abel was not next to Princess Paula. If Princess Paula's cell was not next to Sir Kay, whose cell was?

Clue on page 87.
Answer on page 107.

22. The King's Heir

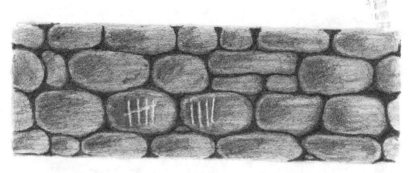

The ogre's prisoners spent a sleepless night in their dungeon cells wondering what fate awaited them. The next morning, the ogre approached the king's sons. "Which one of you is the king's heir?" he demanded.

"I'm Abel, the king's eldest," said the prince with black hair.

"I'm Benjamin, the king's second son," said the one with red hair.

If at least one of them lied, who lied?

23. The Ogre's Boast

"I've devoured more than 100 humans," the ogre boasted.

"Surely, it must be fewer than 100," said Sir Kay.

"Well, I suppose it was at least one," said Abel.

If only one spoke the truth, how many humans did the ogre actually devour?

Clues on pages 87–88.
Answers on pages 108–109.

24. Heads for Hats

Keeping prisoners was much less entertaining than the ogre thought it would be. He decided to have some fun.

The ogre brought in a box with five hats, two red and three white. Then he blindfolded his three young prisoners and placed a hat on each head.

"Each one of you must guess the color of the hat on your own head—without using a mirror," the ogre said in his meanest voice. "I'll take off your blindfolds one by one and let you try. If not one of you guesses correctly, all of you will die."

Abel, the oldest, was used to taking charge. "Don't worry," he said, "I shall save us," and he bid the ogre take off his blindfold first.

He examined the hats his brother and sister were wearing and then admitted that he didn't know what color hat he was wearing.

Benjamin, the second oldest, insisted that he be given the next chance. He, too, was sure that he could save his brother, his sister and himself. But after his blindfold was removed, he, too, had to admit that he did not know the color of the hat he was wearing.

Then Princess Paula said: "I don't need you to take off my blindfold. I can tell you what color hat is on my head."

Did the three go free?

What color hat was Paula wearing?

Clue on page 88.
Answer on pages 109–110.

The Genie's Revenge

Did you know that our twentieth century computers use the number scale of the Australian aborigines and the African pygmies? Two, rather than ten, was probably the basis of our first number system. The solutions to some of the weight puzzles in this chapter hinge on this two scale, others on the three scale.

Weight puzzles first appeared in a collection that was published in France in the 1600's by the mathematician Claude-Gaspar Bachet. They have been baffling puzzle fans ever since.

25. Hidden Gold

The clumsy apprentice of a wealthy Arabian merchant uncorked the jar in which a genie had been imprisoned for many years. Free at last, the genie looked about the Arab's shop to see what mischief he could make. He could, of course, have destroyed the merchant's shop or even killed the merchant, but he quickly realized that the merchant valued his money much more than his life!

Seizing the merchant's gold, he hid it at the bottom of a huge earthen olive jar. Then he brought in eight identical olive jars and placed three-pound weights in them. Last, he filled all the jars with olives and sealed them securely.

When the merchant became distraught at his loss, the genie revealed what he had done and agreed to give the merchant back his wealth if he could guess which jar held the gold. The genie would not let him open any of the jars. He could only weigh them. The catch? He could only use the scale three times.

The merchant owned a balance scale with pans on each side. How did he identify the jar with the gold?

Clue on page 88.
Answer on page 110.

26. Baskets and Baskets

The genie wasn't through with his tricks. In the merchant's warehouse were twelve sealed baskets of grain, one of which was fodder for pigs. The genie stealthily removed the labels and rearranged the baskets so that it was impossible to tell which contained pig fodder.

The merchant didn't discover the situation until a customer arrived to buy four baskets of grain. The important customer was in a hurry. If the pig fodder weighed a bit more than the other grain, how could the merchant, *in one weighing*, avoid the pig fodder and make sure he was selling fine grain?

27. Wanted—Pig Food

The merchant's next customer was a farmer whose storehouse was empty. He needed food for his animals.

How many weighings did it take for the merchant to find the basket of heavier fodder among the group of four baskets he had set aside?

Clues on page 88.
Answers on page 111.

28. Lead Weight

Thwarted by the merchant's ingenuity, the genie spirited away the merchant's scale and weights.

But the merchant made a scale by balancing two empty baskets on either end of a long pole. Then he got a piece of lead weighing exactly 15 ounces.

He cut the bar in four pieces so that he could weigh objects from one to 15 ounces. What were the weights of the four pieces he cut?

29. Heavier Stakes

The merchant still had a problem weighing the heavier merchandise in his bazaar. He bought a 40-pound bar of lead. If he cut the bar into four pieces so that he could weigh items from one pound to 40 pounds, what would each piece have to weigh?

Clues on page 88.
Answers on pages 111–112.

30. Weighty Matters

To weigh a 40-pound object with four weights–1, 3, 9, and 27 pounds—the merchant placed all of the weights on one side of the scale and the object on the other side.

But how did he weigh objects weighing a) 5 pounds? b) 14 pounds? c) 27 pounds? d) 25 pounds?

31. Gold and Silver Coins

The genie was still making his way through the merchant's shop, messing up whatever he could. The merchant had 10 sacks, each containing ten coins. In one sack the coins were silver, in the others gold. The genie slyly coated all the coins bright red and put them back in their original sacks.

The merchant knew that a gold coin weighed 10 grams and that a silver coin weighed a gram less.

If he used a regular scale, how could he determine in one weighing which sack was *not* gold?

Clues on pages 88–89.
Answers on pages 112–113.

Genie Devilment

he puzzles in this chapter may be among the most challenging logic puzzles. We never get quite enough information in these brain-tanglers that pose more than one "if" statement.

Just as in life, we are able to come only to limited conclusions with the information available—and we're likely to mess up unless we're extremely careful about organizing and recording the information we do have.

These classic logic puzzles are tougher, more complex versions of the puzzles in the chapter called "In the Ogre's Dungeon." It's a good idea to work those through before you tackle this chapter.

32. The Brothers Four

Angered at his failure to trick Abou, the merchant, the genie transformed him and his three brothers into animals. He turned one into a pig, one into a donkey, one into a camel, and one into a goat.

1. Ahmed didn't become a pig, and he wasn't a goat.
2. Sharif wasn't a camel, and he wasn't a pig.
3. If Ahmed was not a camel, Omar was not a pig.
4. Abou didn't become a goat, and he was not a pig.
5. Omar was not a goat nor was he a camel.

What did each of the brothers become?

33. Beasts of Burden

Three of the brothers, in their animal guises, were burdened with supplies for the town. They carried either kegs of oil or drums of dates.

1. If the donkey carried dates, then the goat carried oil.
2. If the donkey bore oil, then the camel carried dates.
3. If the goat carried dates, then the camel carried oil.

Whose burden do we know? Who always carried the same load?

Clues on page 89.
Answers on pages 113–114.

34. Feed Bags

Abou, the donkey, had to share a stable and feed bags with a horse and a cow.

1. If Abou ate oats, then the horse ate what the cow ate.
2. If the horse ate oats, then Abou ate what the cow did not eat.
3. If the cow ate hay, then Abou ate what the horse ate.

Who always ate from the same feed bag?

Clue on page 90.
Answer on pages 115–116.

Magic Numbers

After ten years, the wives of Abou and his brothers appealed to the genie.

"Sire, we beg you," said Sharif's wife. "Our husbands have suffered enough. And our children need their fathers."

The genie agreed to transform the brothers back to their human forms, but only if the wives could give him three magic numbers which met certain conditions.

35. The First Magic Number

Here are the conditions of the first number:

A. If the first magic number was a multiple of 2, then it was a number from 50 through 59.
B. If it was not a multiple of 3, then it was a number from 60 through 69.
C. If the first magic number was not a multiple of 4, then it was a number from 70 through 79.

What was the first magic number?

Clue on page 90.
Answer on pages 116–117.

36. The Second Magic Number

Here are the conditions of the second number:

A. If the second magic number was a multiple of 6, then it was a number from 40 through 49.
B. If it was not a multiple of 7, then it was a number from 60 through 69.
C. If the second magic number was not a multiple of 8, then it was a number from 80 through 89.

What was the second magic number?

37. The Third Magic Number

Here are the conditions of the third number:

A. If the third magic number was a multiple of 7, then it was a number from 30 through 39.
B. If it was not a multiple of 9, then it was a number from 40 through 49.
C. If the third magic number was not a multiple of 11, then it was a number from 60 through 69.

What was the third magic number?

Clues on page 90.
Answers on page 117.

The Dragon Montagne

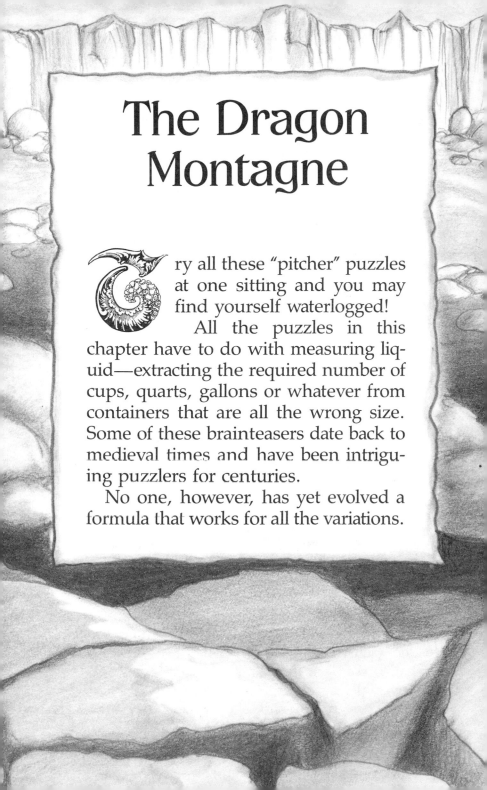

ry all these "pitcher" puzzles at one sitting and you may find yourself waterlogged!

All the puzzles in this chapter have to do with measuring liquid—extracting the required number of cups, quarts, gallons or whatever from containers that are all the wrong size. Some of these brainteasers date back to medieval times and have been intriguing puzzlers for centuries.

No one, however, has yet evolved a formula that works for all the variations.

38. Seth Meets the Dragon

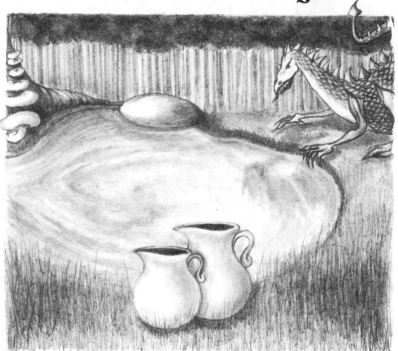

Princess Fleur travelled to a distant mountain pool to sample its waters. There she and her retinue were captured by the terrible dragon Montagne, who had taken over the entire countryside. When word got back to the king, he offered half his wealth and the princess in marriage to anyone who could rescue her and defeat the dragon.

One after another, the knights of the kingdom set forth. But each in turn failed.

One day, Seth, a young peasant lad, went to face the dreaded monster. "My village is hungry and thirsty," Seth said. "We need the water you guard."

"Seven times seven knights have failed to solve my seven puzzles and are now my prisoners," said the dragon Montagne, breathing out flames. "Would you be foolish, too?"

"I'm only an ignorant peasant, not a knight," said Seth. "But I'll try."

"Be prepared for the consequences!" thundered the dragon. "First, measure out exactly four cups of the water in the pond using only these pitchers."

The dragon swished his tail and two pitchers appeared. Seth picked them up. Neither measured four cups. One could hold exactly three cups and the other exactly five cups.

Seth, however, worked on a farm.

How does he measure out exactly four cups and thus complete the first task?

39. The Second Challenge

"That was just the first task," hissed the dragon angrily.

With a swish of his tail he dried up the mountain pond and made the two pitchers vanish. Suddenly three new pitchers appeared, a 5-cup, a 7-cup, and a 12-cup pitcher. Then the dragon snorted and the 12-cup pitcher was filled with water. The 5-cup pitcher and the 7-cup pitcher remained empty.

"Divide the water in the 12-cup pitcher into two equal parts!" he challenged.

How does Seth do it?

Clues on page 90.
Answers on pages 117–119.

40. The Three Steps

The dragon Montagne breathed a bolt of fire. This time three jugs appeared. One of them, an eight-litre jug, was filled with water. The other two jugs, one measuring three litres and one measuring two litres, were empty.

"Give me back four litres—in three steps," the dragon roared.

And, in three steps, Seth gives him back four litres. How?

Clue on pages 90–91.
Answer on pages 119–120.

41. Wicked Walter

What no one knew was that the dragon Montagne was really the wicked apprentice wizard Walter in disguise. He had great natural talent as a wizard, fooling the entire kingdom with his dragon act, but so far the only things Walter had learned to conjure up were containers, and the only puzzles he knew had to do with measuring water. He didn't have power over anyone who could solve his puzzles, and though he feared Seth would continue to succeed where others had failed, he desperately continued with his bluff.

Walter (as the dragon) conjured up three urns. One contained ten gallons of water. The other two were empty, one capable of holding four gallons, and the other three gallons.

"Give me back five gallons, using only five steps," Walter demanded of Seth.

Clue on page 91.
Answer on page 120.

42. Drop by Drop

Snarling, Wicked Walter (as the dragon) materialized two vials so small that Seth could place them both on one finger. One vial could hold five drops of liquid and the other seven drops.

"What is the least number of steps it will take to give me three drops of water, and what is the least number of steps it will take to give me four drops of water?" challenged the dragon.

"Aren't you giving me two puzzles?" protested Seth.

Walter snorted fiercely. Seth set about solving the problems.

How?

43. Triple Threat

For the next challenge, Wicked Walter placed before Seth four jars, the largest of which held nine litres of water. The three empty jars could hold five, four and two litres respectively.

"This time," Walter said: "You are to divide nine litres into three equal parts."

How many steps does it take Seth this time?

Clues on page 91.
Answers on pages 120–122.

44. The Rescue

For the final challenge, Walter, the dragon Montagne, presented Seth with two 10-gallon vats full of water and two pitchers, one holding five pints and the other holding four pints.

"Place one quart in each pitcher," Walter said.

After several hours, Seth wearily presented the dragon with a quart in each pitcher, whereupon the dragon Montagne was revealed to all as the Wicked Walter. He had no choice but to free Princess Fleur, her ladies-in-waiting, her pages, and the forty-nine knights who had sought to rescue her.

How does Seth solve this last puzzle and expose Wicked Walter?

Clue on page 91.
Answer on page 122.

The Wizards of Odds

hat are the odds? How do you determine your chances of winning?

All the puzzles in this chapter deal with figuring the odds, a concept that is said to have originated in the 17th century. The story goes like this: Two gamblers were interrupted during a game of chance and weren't able to finish playing. They needed to split up the money they had bet, but they couldn't figure out how. Finally, they asked a mathematician friend, Blaise Pascal, to settle the matter. Pascal and his colleague, Pierre de Fermat, came up with a formula that indicated how things *probably* would have turned out if the game had been completed.

From these frivolous roots developed the theory of probability that has be-

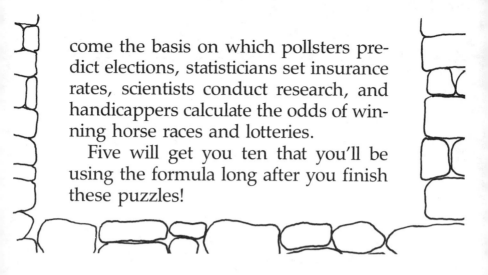

come the basis on which pollsters predict elections, statisticians set insurance rates, scientists conduct research, and handicappers calculate the odds of winning horse races and lotteries.

Five will get you ten that you'll be using the formula long after you finish these puzzles!

45. The Well of Wisdom

Once a year apprentice wizards, witches, sorcerers, and sorceresses come from many different kingdoms to a conference at which they learn about new potions and omens.

This year they meet in the kingdom Merlin serves as Chief Wizard. Of the thirty apprentices he invites, only two are unable to attend, having been wounded fighting off a sudden influx of dragons.

As the apprentices come in, Merlin gives them each a gold coin to toss into the Well of Wisdom. If the toss of the coin matches the previous toss—whether it was heads or tails—the apprentice who pitches it will acquire a new power.

Wizard Merlin will toss the first gold coin. What chance is there that it will come up heads?

Clue on page 91.
Answer on pages 122–123.

46. Evelynne at the Well

The first guest to arrive is Evelynne, apprenticed to the Lady of the Lake. What is the probability that Merlin's and Evelynne's tosses both come up heads?

47. And Percival Makes Three

Percival, aide to the Wizard of the Woods, tosses the next coin. What is the probability that all three coins will come up heads?

48. Four Coins in the Well

Vivienne, student of the Woodland Sorcerer, tosses fourth. What are the odds for heads coming up in all four tosses?

49. Oberon's Toss

Suppose Vivienne's coin comes up tails. What are the chances that Oberon's coin, tossed right after Vivienne's, comes up tails?

Clues on pages 91–92.
Answers on pages 123–125.

50. How Many Wiser Wizards?

How many of the twenty-eight apprentices are likely to match the previous toss and acquire the new power Merlin promised?

51. Magic Seeds

Merlin passes around an urn of new black and white magic seeds to the budding wizards and witches for them to sample. The magician who developed them claims that the black seed makes one impervious to dragon fire and that the white seed provides the cloak of invisibility.

The urn dispenses one seed to each apprentice sorcerer. By the time it reaches Titania and Garth of Glend there are only two black seeds and one white seed left.

What is the probability of both getting a black seed?

Clues on page 92.
Answers on page 125.

52. Blind Sorcerer's Buff

Merlin singles out four of the apprentice sorcerers and asks each one to stand at a corner of the huge ballroom in the castle. He blindfolds them and steers them to the middle of the room. Then he turns each around several times and tells them to return to their original corners.

If each one winds up in a corner, what is the probability that all four will succeed in getting back to the right one?

53. Encore

To vary the challenge, Merlin blindfolds another four apprentices and sets them in the four corners of the ballroom. Then he steers them, blindfolded, to the middle of the room, directing them to return to their original corners one at a time. Once a corner is occupied, it is off bounds.

If each one reaches a corner, what are the odds that these four apprentices will return to their original corners?

Clues on page 92.
Answers on page 125.

54. Non-Magic Magic

Merlin calls on two of the apprentice sorcerers to entertain with magic tricks using an ordinary deck of cards. Unfortunately, neither apprentice has practised enough to be very good at card tricks. They are at the mercy of the laws of chance.

If each one pulls a card at random from a deck of 52 cards, who has the better chance of being a successful magician: Lorelei, who promises to come up with one of the four aces? Or Urth, who claims his first card will be one of the 13 hearts?

Clues on page 92.
Answer on pages 125–126.

55. More Card Tricks

Will Lorelei have a better chance of coming up with two aces if she returns the first ace she draws to the deck or if she puts it aside?

56. Hearts for Urth

Will Urth have a better chance of coming up with two hearts if he returns the first heart to the deck or if he puts it aside?

57. Go Fish

Merlin provides some fun by stocking the castle pond with a fish for each guest. Two of the thirty fish he endows with enchantment.

The student wizards and sorcerers take turns casting.

Does Pendragon, apprentice to the not-so-wily wizard of Trelawn, have a better chance of luring an enchanted fish if he goes first or if he casts tenth and one enchanted fish has already been caught?

58. Two Enchanted Fish?

What are the chances that Pendragon and Elaine of Camelot both get enchanted fish?

Clues on page 92.
Answers on page 126.

Magic Forces

hat next?

Powerful forces and strong magic are at work in these puzzles. Look at the changing pictures carefully. From the pattern of what has happened before, you'll be able to indicate what will happen next—to predict the future.

There are no clues and few words in this chapter.

59. Martian Locomotion

Scientists Bruce and Audrey Mann conduct a briefing for the explorers to prepare them for what they will encounter as they travel in space and time. They show pictures of the Martians and others in various situations, and ask the adventurers—and us—to predict what will happen next.

This is how the Martians move:

What happens next? Choose one:

A   B   C   D

Answer on page 126.

60. The Dragon's Pitchers

When the dragon swished its tail, only four pitchers appeared instead of five.

Which pitcher is missing?

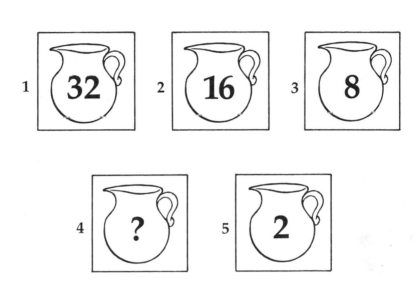

Choose one:

Answer on page 126.

61. Merlin Waves a Wand

Merlin waves his wand and mysterious things happen.

Before

After

Which of the following (A through D) happens next?

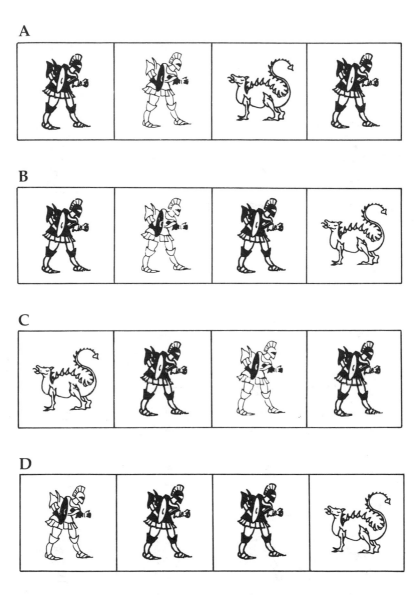

Answer on page 126.

62. Martian Manners

The finned and feathered groups on Mars are not always on the best of terms. This is what sometimes happens when they are together:

Before

After

Before

After

Before

What happens next? Choose from A through D.

A

B

C

D

Answer on page 126.

63. Knights and Their Weapons

Always preparing for combat, the knights practise with their weapons, like this:

Before

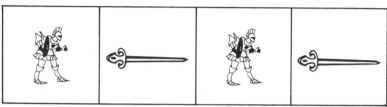

After

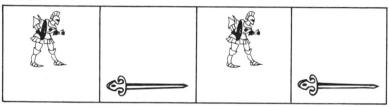

And like this:

Before

After

This is the way things are now:

What happens next? Choose from A through D.

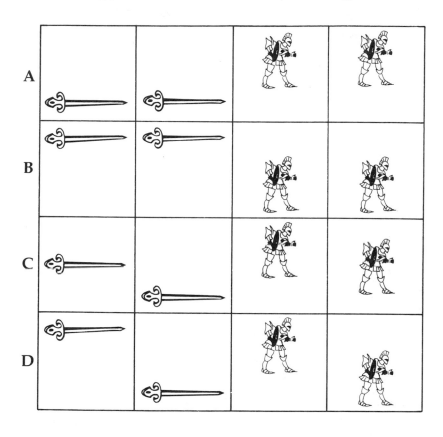

Answer on page 127.

64. The Missing Swords

Decorating the walls of the Wizard Zorn's secret laboratory are sets of swords, each with different magic powers. One day, to his dismay, a rival sorcerer steals in and spirits away a set of Zorn's most potent weapons.

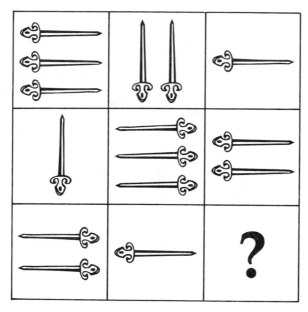

Which swords are missing?

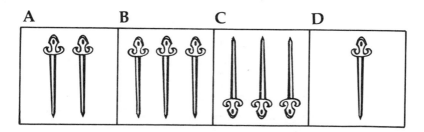

Answer on page 127.

65. The Genie and the Coins

How many coins were there in the sack the genie hid?

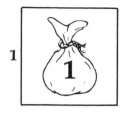  

Choose one:

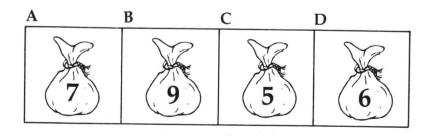

Answer on page 127.

66. Genie Power

The genie is having a field day, getting revenge on men and animals alike. What is he doing to them?

Before

After

Before

After

This is the way things are now:

What happens next? Choose from A through D.

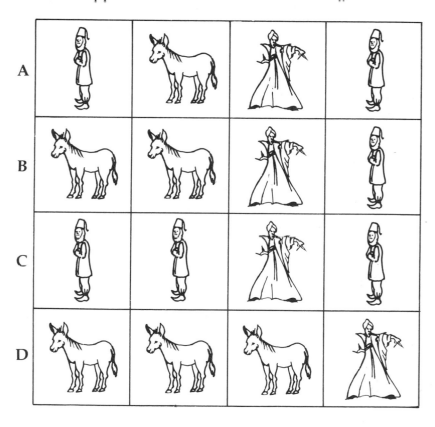

Answer on page 127.

67. Genie Horseplay

What is the genie doing to the merchant's horses?

Before

After

Before

After

Here is how things are now:

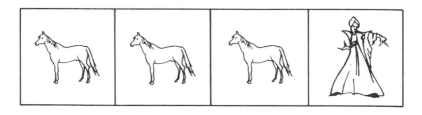

What happens next? Choose from A through D.

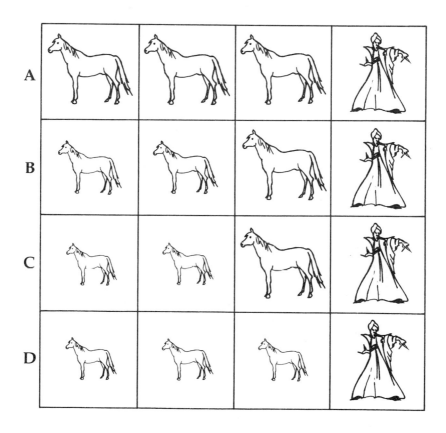

Answer on page 127.

68. Martian Square Dance

Before formal meetings, members of some Martian groups participate in a ceremonial dance. If the dance continues as it started, what will be the next move?

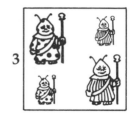

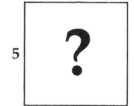

Choose one:

A   B   C   D

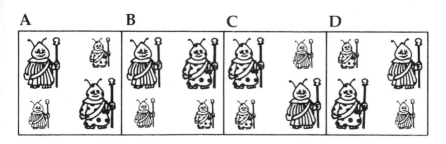

Answer on page 127.

69. Genie Hijinks

To entertain himself, a genie sets things whirling.

What happens next? Choose from A to D.

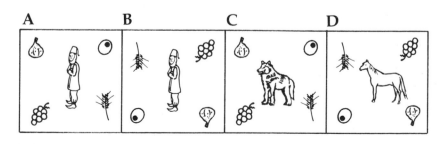

Answer on page 127.

70. Medieval Merry-Go-Round

A powerful wizard has created a spectacular illusion to entertain his guests. The images he has conjured up are spinning in a circle.

What happens next?

Choose one:

A   B   C   D

Answer on page 127.

1. The Martian Rub: Mark must ask something that will surely get the Martian to answer yes.

2. Stone Stew: Pay attention to the wording: The sacks were *all* mislabelled.

3. Friend or Foe?: Whether he was a truth-teller or a liar, the striped Martian's answer would be the same.

4. How Many Liars?: Whether the finned Martian was a truth-teller or not, he would have said he was a truth-teller.

5. The Search for Doman: Find out which one belongs to the Uti, the truth-tellers.

6. Martian Mystery: Each Grundi made only *one* false statement. Look for the statements that must be true, and for the contradictions.

7. Tsientsien Don't Eat: Try using different coins (a dime, a nickel and a penny, for instance) to represent the various specimens and make the trips with them. Some may have to make more than one trip.

8. The Gravity on Mars: Try coins again or two pairs of matches, one cut in half, to make the trips across the water.

9. Rockfall: Make the crossings with three pennies representing the Grundi and three quarters representing the Earthlings. Remember that there never can be more pennies than quarters on either side of the river.

10. Fins and Feathers: Try using three different coins (two pennies, two nickels and two dimes, perhaps) to represent each of the three Martian groups. Place one of each type of coin heads up: these are the three feathered Martians.

Place the other three coins tails up: these are the finned Martians. Then take them across the ravine, but remember that no head may stay alone with a tail of a different coin.

11. Flying Teams: With the help of a grid, you can use the process of elimination to determine who is not the Uti and, therefore, who is.

	Uti	Grundi	Yomi
Rir			
Vel			
Pyi			
Teta			
Wora			
Xera			

12. Spaceship Crew: This is a classic puzzle and not nearly so difficult as it looks. Notice that the astronauts, but not the Martians, have first names.

Set up two grids.

	Uti	Grundi	Yomi
Jones			
Robinson			
Smith			

	Jones	Robinson	Smith
Engineer			
Biochemist			
Pilot			

13. A Flock of Martians: Three grids will be helpful.

	Uti	Grundi	Yomi	Rafi
Aken				
Bal				
Mun				
Wora				

	Red	Green	Blue	Brown
Aken				
Bal				
Mun				
Wora				

	Red	Green	Blue	Brown
Uti				
Grundi				
Yomi				
Rafi				

14. Aken's Friend: Draw two tables and provide eight chairs for each. Fill the seats of one with the names of the guests. Fill the seats of the other with their characteristics.

15. In the Dark: Don't get confused by the number of boots he owned. There were just two *types*.

16. Sword Play: Ignore the number of weapons and focus on the number of *types* of weapons.

17. Royal Dinner: Take into account not only the number of patterns but the number of guests.

18. Anti-Ogre Potions: The kind of potion the princes get is important since they are bent on fighting an ogre, not a dragon or a wizard.

19. Seven-League Boots: Refer back to the last puzzle, #18, "Anti-Ogre Potions."

20. In the Forest: Take one statement at a time and make the comparisons.

21. Captured!: Draw the cells and the people in them so that no statement is contradictory.

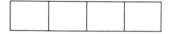

22. The King's Heir: Consider the possible true-false combinations:

	1	2	3	4
Black Hair	T	T	F	F
Red Hair	T	F	T	F

23. The Ogre's Boast: Which statements are not possible? Which statements contradict one another? Use the following "truth table" to organize the possibilities:

	A	B	C	D	E	F	G	H
Ogre	T	T	T	T	F	F	F	F
Kay	T	T	F	F	T	T	F	F
Abel	T	F	F	T	T	F	T	F

24. Heads for Hats: Since there were only two red hats, both Benjamin and Paula could not both have been wearing red hats or Abel would have known he was wearing a white hat. Therefore, either Benjamin and Paula were both wearing white hats, or one was wearing a red and one a white hat.

25. Hidden Gold: Divide the jars into groups of three.

26. Baskets and Baskets: Divide the baskets into groups of four.

27. Wanted—Pig Food: Consider how to divide the four baskets in order to weigh them.

28. Lead Weight: The solution lies in using the binary system, the scale of two, rather than the decimal system.

29. Heavier Stakes: Instead of using either the decimal system or the binary system, use a base of three. And remember, weights can be placed in the pan on either side of the scale.

30. Weighty Matters: When you place a weight on the same pan of the scale as the object you are weighing, you subtract that weight from the total of the weights on the pan on the other side.

31. Gold and Silver Coins: Line up the sacks of coins and number them from 1 to 10.

32. The Brothers Four: Set up a grid with the possibilities.

	Pig	Donkey	Camel	Goat
Ahmed				
Sharif				
Abou				
Omar				

The conditional situation appears in Statement 3, in the "if" clause, which permits three possibilities (one if the hypothesis, the "if" clause, is true and two if it is false):

   A. Ahmed was not a camel, and Omar was not a pig.
   B. Ahmed was a camel, and Omar was not a pig.
   C. Ahmed was a camel, and Omar was a pig.

33. Beasts of Burden: With three animals involved, there are eight possibilities. Make a table itemizing them, such as the following:

	A	B	C	D	E	F	G	H
Donkey	o	o	o	o	d	d	d	d
Goat	o	o	d	d	o	o	d	d
Camel	o	d	o	d	o	d	o	d

Then determine which possibilities are incompatible with the conditional statements.

34. Feed Bags: Set up a table of the eight possibilities:

	A	B	C	D	E	F	G	H
Abou	O	O	O	O	H	H	H	H
Horse	O	O	H	H	O	O	H	H
Cow	O	H	O	H	O	H	O	H

35–37. Magic Numbers: For each of the magic numbers, make a chart involving all of the possible numbers, such as the following for the first magic number.

50	51	52	53	54	55	56	57	58	59
60	61	62	63	64	65	66	67	68	69
70	71	72	73	74	75	76	77	78	79

Cross out those numbers that contradict any of the statements.

38. Seth Meets the Dragon: Lining up the pitchers next to the pond, create a chart:

Pond   5-Cup Pitcher   3-Cup Pitcher

Start by filling either pitcher and then pouring the water from one to the other and back into the pond.

39. The Second Challenge: No pond this time, but three pitchers to line up:

12-Cup Pitcher   7-Cup Pitcher   5-Cup Pitcher

40. The Three Steps: Consider which approach involves fewer steps—pouring first into the 3-litre or into the 2-litre jug.

	A.	8-Litre Jug	3-Litre Jug	2-Litre Jug	
		8	0	0	
1.		6	0	2	And so on.

or **B.**

8-Litre Jug	3-Litre Jug	2-Litre Jug	
	8	0	0
1.	5	3	0	And so on.

41. Wicked Walter: Gallons or cups, the approach is the same. Line up the containers and pour from one to the other. But which approach results in only five steps— pouring first into the 4-gallon urn or into the 3-gallon urn?

A.

10-Gallon Urn	4-Gallon Urn	3-Gallon Urn	
	10	0	0
1.	6	4	0	And so on.

Or:

B.

10-Gallon Urn	4-Gallon Urn	3-Gallon Urn	
	10	0	0
1.	7	0	3	And so on.

42. Drop by Drop: Figure out which to fill first, the smaller or the larger, to get the exact amount in the fewest possible steps.

43. Triple Threat: Line up the four jars. How many litres should be in each jar when the water is divided among three?

9-Pint Jar	5-Pint Jar	4-Pint Jar	2-Pint Jar	
	9	0	0	0
1.	4	5	0	0	And so on.

44. The Rescue: Line up the four containers. Convert the gallons into pints. (1 gallon = 4 quarts; 1 quart = 2 pints.)

45. The Well of Wisdom: Assuming that the coin doesn't roll on its edge, how many ways *can* it land?

46. Evelynne at the Well: Chart the possibilities.

47. And Percival Makes Three: How many combinations can there be? No, *not* 6!

48. Four Coins in the Well: You can still list the possibilities, but now it is far easier to use the formula.

49. Oberon's Toss: Don't fall into a trap. Vivienne's coin has already come up tails.

50. How Many Wiser Wizards?: Each play has one chance in two of matching the previous toss.

51. Magic Seeds: How many possibilities are there for Titania to get a black seed? How many possibilities for Garth if Titania draws a black seed? What is the formula?

52. Blind Sorcerer's Buff: How many possibilities are involved for each one? Remember the formula? (See "Evelynne at the Well" solution, page 123.)

53. Encore: For the apprentice who starts first, the odds are one in four. But what about the others?

54. Non-Magic Magic: Remember the Magic Seeds solution? (See page 125.)

55. More Card Tricks: Compare the odds in each instance, using the joint occurrence formula. (See page 123.)

56. Hearts for Urth: Again, compare the odds using the joint recurrence formula.

57. Go Fish: Consider the mathematics in each situation.

58. Two Enchanted Fish?: Look to the joint recurrence formula again.

No clues for puzzles 59–70.

1. The Martian Rub: Mark rubbed his stomach and asked, "Did you do this?" Whatever the Martian did in reply would mean yes.

2. Stone Stew: One rock from one sack. If he were to open the sack labelled "igneous," for instance, and the rock turned out to be sedimentary, then he would know that the other two sacks *could not* contain sedimentary rocks. The other sacks then would have either igneous or metamorphic rocks in them. Since *all* the sacks were mislabelled, the one labelled "sedimentary" must then contain metamorphic and the one labelled "metamorphic" must contain igneous rocks.

"Stone Stew" is not exactly a truth puzzle, but it is included because it does involve being misled. It points out the need for careful attention to the language of a puzzle. Most people are stuck until they reread it, and then they're amazed at how they could have had such trouble.

3. Friend or Foe: The spotted Martian. Truth-teller or not, the striped Martian would answer yes. Why? If he were a truth-teller, obviously he would tell the truth and say yes. If he were a liar, he would lie and say yes. Therefore, since the spotted Martian said that the striped Martian would say yes, he *must be* the truth-teller, and the striped Martian must be the liar.

4. How Many Liars? One. Since the finned Martian did indicate that he was a truth-teller, then the Martian with feathered ears was obviously telling the truth and must be a truth-teller. If the finned Martian was lying, then the horned Martian was a truth-teller. If the finned Martian was a truth-teller, then the horned Martian was a liar. So, no matter how you look at it, two of the three Martians were truth-tellers and one was a liar.

5. The Search for Doman: He is a Uti.

1. Aken said he was not a Uti. If he were a Uti, he couldn't say he was not one since Uti always tell the truth. So he is definitely not a Uti. If he were a Yomi he couldn't say he was *not* a Uti since that would be the truth and the Yomi always lie. So he cannot be a Yomi. Therefore, Aken is a Grundi who sometimes tells the truth and sometimes lies. And so we still don't know what group Doman belongs to.
2. Bal said he was not a Yomi. But is he a lying Yomi or a truth-telling Uti? We don't know yet.
3. Cwos said he was not a Grundi. Since each of the three Martians belongs to a different group, and we already know that Aken is the only Grundi among them, Cwos must be telling the truth. Therefore Cwos is a Uti.
4. It follows that Bal must be a Yomi, because he lied by denying that he is a Yomi.
5. Since Cwos is the truth-teller, Doman must be a Uti because Cwos said he is.

6. Martian Mystery: Uk.

1. Tset said (in his first statement) that he did not throw the rock and (in his third statement) that Zum lied by saying he, Tset, did. Since only one of the three statements could be false, both of these must be true. Therefore, his second statement that Yan did it must be a lie. So, we know that both Tset and Yan are innocent.
2. Zum said that Tset did it, and so we know that this statement is Zum's one lie. Therefore, Zum's statement, "I am innocent," is the truth.
   Who is left as a possible culprit? Pala and Uk.
3. Since Tset is innocent, Pala's comment that Tset did it was her lie. Therefore, her statements that she was innocent and that she never saw Yan before were true.
4. Yan's assertion that he and Pala were old friends was therefore a lie. He told the truth when he said that he, Yan, was innocent and that Uk was guilty.

7. Tsientsien Don't Eat:
1. Mark took the farfel to the aircraft and left it there.
2. He drove back alone.
3. He transported the tsientsien and left it there.
4. He drove back with the farfel.
5. He transported the garble and left it there with the tsientsien.
6. He drove back alone.
7. He transported the farfel.

8. The Gravity on Mars:
1. Two Martians crossed.
2. One Martian paddled back.
3. One Earthling crossed.
4. The other Martian paddled back.
5. Two Martians crossed.
6. One Martian paddled back.
7. The second Earthling crossed.
8. The second Martian paddled back.
9. The two Martians crossed.

9. Rockfall:
1. One Earthling took one Grundi across (leaving two Earthlings and two Grundi on the west side).
2. One Earthling returned (leaving one Grundi east).
3. Two Grundi crossed (leaving three Earthlings west).
4. One Grundi returned (leaving two Grundi east).
5. Two Earthlings crossed (leaving one Grundi and one Earthling on the west).
6. One Grundi and one Earthling returned (leaving one Grundi and one Earthling on the east side).
7. Two Earthlings crossed (leaving two Grundi west).
8. One Grundi returned (leaving three Earthlings east).
9. Two Grundi crossed (leaving one Grundi west).
10. One Grundi came back (leaving three Earthlings and one Grundi on the east side).
11. Two Grundi crossed (no one left in danger).

10. Fins and Feathers:

1. Uti finned and Uti feathered swung over.
2. Uti finned returned.
3. Grundi feathered and Grundi finned swung over.
4. Uti feathered returned.
5. Yomi feathered and Yomi finned swung over.
6. Grundi finned returned.
7. Uti feathered and Uti finned swung over.
8. Uti finned returned.
9. Uti finned and Grundi finned returned.

11. Flying Teams: Wora and Pyi.

1. From statement 6, we can assume that Xera and Rir come from different groups since they would have known one another if they were on the team from the same group.
2. From statement 7, we learn that Xera is a Yomi.
3. Therefore neither Rir, who comes from another group, nor Pyi, whom she will visit, comes from Yomi territory.
4. Since each team has one male on it, Vel, the only one left, must be the male who is a Yomi.

	Uti	Grundi	Yomi
Rir			N
Vel	N	N	Y
Pyi			N
Teta			
Wora			
Xera	N	N	Y

5. Since Xera is a Yomi, either Teta or Wora must be the female on the Uti team.
6. But, from statements 5 and 8, we learn that Teta's home is the land of the Grundi.

7. Therefore, Wora must be a Uti.

	Uti	Grundi	Yomi
Rir			N
Vel	N	N	Y
Pyi			N
Teta	N	Y	N
Wora	Y	N	N
Xera	N	N	Y

8. Also from statement 8, we learn that Pyi admires Teta and her teammate and therefore cannot be her team-mate nor be a Grundi.

	Uti	Grundi	Yomi
Rir			N
Vel	N	N	Y
Pyi	Y	N	N
Teta	N	Y	N
Wora	Y	N	N
Xera	N	N	Y

Then Pyi must be Wora's Uti teammate.
Wora and Pyi are the winners.

12. Spaceship Crew: Jan Robinson.
1. In statement 1, we are told that Robinson is a Yomi.
2. From statement 2, which tells us that Jones doesn't speak any language other than Martian, and 3, which tells us that the Uti are linguists, we can infer that Jones is not a Uti.

3. Since Robinson is a Yomi and Jones can't speak anything other than Martian, it follows then that the Uti who serves as interpreter must be Smith.

	Uti	Grundi	Yomi
Jones	N		N
Robinson	N	N	Y
Smith	Y	N	N

4. We also infer, from 4, that the biochemist's name can't be Smith since Smith, the interpreter, admires the Martian with the same name as the biochemist. The biochemist's name must then be either Robinson or Jones.
5. But we can learn from statement 5 that the biochemist's name is the same as the Grundi's. It is, therefore, Jones.

	Jones	Robinson	Smith
Engineer	N		
Biochemist	Y	N	N
Pilot	N		

6. In the last statement, we learn that Jan Robinson beat the engineer at chess. Therefore, Jan Robinson is neither the biochemist who is named Jones nor the engineer whom she beat.

	Jones	Robinson	Smith
Engineer	N	N	
Biochemist	Y	N	N
Pilot	N		

Jan Robinson must be the pilot.

13. A Flock of Martians: Mun, the Rafi.

1. From statement 1, we know that the Uti ate breakfast with Mun. Therefore, Mun can't be a Uti.

2. In statement 2, we are told that Bal and the Yomi debated. And so Bal isn't the Yomi.

	Uti	Grundi	Yomi	Rafi
Aken				
Bal			N	
Mun	N			
Wora				

3. From 2, we can infer that Bal doesn't have either blue or brown feathers since we are told Bal and the Yomi debated and fought with them.

	Red	Green	Blue	Brown
Aken				
Bal			N	N
Mun				
Wora				

4. Also from 2, we know that the Yomi doesn't have blue or brown feathers.

	Red	Green	Blue	Brown
Uti				
Grundi				
Yomi			N	N
Rafi				

5. From 3, we know that Wora is not the one who has brown feathers since Wora and the Rafi seconded that diplomat's arguments.

	Red	Green	Blue	Brown
Aken				
Bal			N	N
Mun				
Wora				N

6. From 3, we also know that the Rafi is not the Martian with brown feathers.

	Red	Green	Blue	Brown
Uti				
Grundi				
Yomi			N	N
Rafi				N

7. From 3 also, since she didn't agree with her, we know Wora is not the Grundi.

	Uti	Grundi	Yomi	Rafi
Aken				
Bal			N	
Mun	N			
Wora		N		

8. In 3, we are told that the Grundi has red feathers.

	Red	Green	Blue	Brown
Uti	N			
Grundi	Y			
Yomi	N		N	N
Rafi	N			N

9. Obviously the Yomi must be green-feathered, since all the other possibilities have been eliminated.
10. With the same reasoning, the Rafi must be the one with blue feathers. And since it is the only possibility left, the brown-feathered Martian is the Uti.

	Red	Green	Blue	Brown
Uti	N	N	N	
Grundi	Y	N	N	N
Yomi	N	Y	N	N
Rafi	N	N	Y	N

Now that we know the color of feathers of each group, we can determine their names.

11. Since Bal debated with the Yomi, she could be a Uti, a Grundi or a Rafi. But she debated and fought with the blue-feathered Martian, the Rafi, and the brown, the Uti. Therefore, she must be the red-feathered Grundi.

	Uti	Grundi	Yomi	Rafi
Aken				
Bal	N	Y	N	N
Mun	N			
Wora		N	Y	N

12. Even before we learned that Bal had red feathers, we knew from 3 that Wora was not the red-feathered Grundi. In 3, we are also told that Wora and the Rafi admired the brown-feathered Martian. So Wora is neither the brown-feathered Uti nor the blue-feathered Rafi. She must be a green-feathered Yomi.

	Uti	Grundi	Yomi	Rafi
Aken		N	N	
Bal	N	Y	N	N
Mun	N	N	N	
Wora	N	N	Y	N

	Red	Green	Blue	Brown
Uti	N	N	N	Y
Grundi	Y	N	N	N
Yomi	N	Y	N	N
Rafi	N	N	Y	N

13. Mun is therefore the Rafi, the one in blue feathers.

14. Aken's Friend: Rider is Aken's friend.

1. Aken's friend is not Mark who, we learn in statement 1, is sitting opposite him.

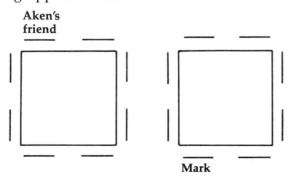

103

2. It can't be Wora who, according to 2, is sitting between the math whiz and Aken's friend and, according to 3, opposite the tall one.

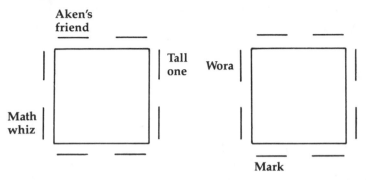

3. Aken's friend cannot be Aken of course, who, also according to statement 3, is sitting to left of the tall one.
4. Mun, described in 4, was obviously the tall one who, according to 3, sat opposite Wora and to the right of Aken.
5. According to statement 4, it can't be Smith, who had no friends among the group and sat to the right of Mun.

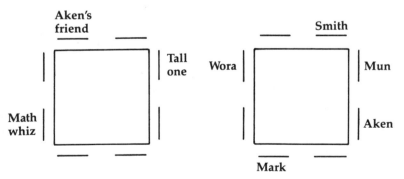

6. In statement 5, we learn that the one with yellow feathers sat between Mun and the one who spoke many languages, and opposite Bal. Therefore, the one with yellow feathers was Aken. And Bal was the math whiz and not Aken's friend.

7. Who is left? Only Jones or Rider can be Aken's friend. Statement 6 tells us that Jones was to the right of the rock collector and opposite the pilot who was next to Rider. But Aken's friend was opposite Mark and so Jones could not be Aken's friend.

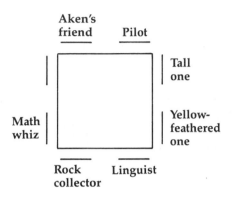

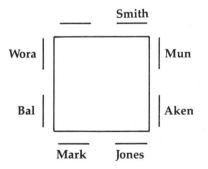

8. Rider is Aken's friend.

15. In the Dark: Three. If the ogre pulled out only two boots, he might have had to wear one six-league and one seven-league boot. He took out three because at least two of the three would have to be the same type. The formula: $N + 1$ (N represents the number of types). $2 + 1 = 3$.

16. Sword Play: Four. The formula again: N + 1 (with N representing the types of ogre-fighters). If the swordsmith had pulled out two or three, he might have picked one of each type. Since he had only three types of weapons, with four he would have at least two of one type. He had three types of weapons and so N = 3. 3 + 1 = 4.

17. Royal Dinner: Ten. Though, by chance, she might have taken down four matching plates, consider the possibilities if the queen had taken down the following number of plates:

4 might have resulted in 2, 1, 1
5 might have resulted in 2, 2, 1
6 might have resulted in 2, 2, 2
7 might have resulted in 3, 2, 2
8 might have resulted in 3, 3, 2
9 might have resulted in 3, 3, 3

Only with ten, would it be inevitable that she would have at least four of any one pattern: 3, 3, 4.

In order to ensure matching plates, the queen had to bring down three extra plates, one for each pattern, for each person more than two.

The formula: N + 1 + N(X) (with N representing the number of patterns or types and X representing the number of people more than two).

The queen had three patterns of plates and so N = 3. In addition to the king and queen, there were two guests, and so X = 2.   3 + 1 + 3(2) = 10.

Try it and you will find that for three persons the queen would have needed to take down seven plates, and for five she would have had to take down 13 plates.

If her children had not been out ogre-fighting, the royal queen might have had to mix and match!

18. Anti-Ogre Potions: Seven. If the wizard took out four potions, he certainly would have two of the same kind, but not necessarily the ogre-fighters. He could have two of the evil wizard-vanquishers or the dragon-destroyers. And what good would they be in combat with an ogre?

If he took out five potions, he might wind up with three dragon-destroyers, two evil wizard-vanquishers, and no ogre-fighters. If he grabbed for six potions, they might include three dragon-destroyers, two wizard-vanquishers, and one ogre-fighter. But if he took out seven, he would have to have at least two ogre-fighters, since only five other potions are not ogre-fighters.

19. Seven-League Boots: Six. Since he had only four six-league boots, if he took out six boots, he'd have at least one pair of seven-league boots.

20. In the Forest: Prince Benjamin. We know that Sir Kay shot down more than Princess Paula (statement 1), and that Prince Benjamin captured more than Sir Kay (statement 2). Therefore, Prince Benjamin captured more than either Sir Kay or Princess Paula.

In addition, we know that Princess Paula hit more than Prince Abel (statement 3). Therefore, Prince Benjamin was more successful than Sir Kay, Paula or Abel.

21. Captured!: Prince Abel's.

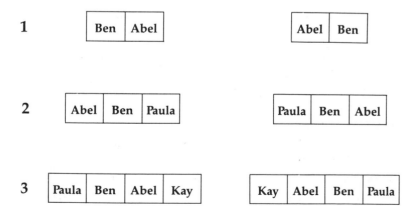

22. The King's Heir: Both lied.

If you read the puzzle carefully, you'll see that the answer is obvious and that the puzzle doesn't require the involved solution that follows. It is included here only as an easy introduction to the method that is useful for more difficult puzzles.

	1	2	3	4
Black Hair	T	T	F	F
Red Hair	T	F	T	F

1. The first possibility indicates both princes were telling the truth. But we were told that at least one of them was lying.
2. We can eliminate both 2 and 3 because if either lied, the other could not have spoken the truth.

   If the prince with black hair lied when he said he was Abel, then he was Benjamin and the other prince must have been Abel.

   If the prince with red hair lied when he said he was Benjamin, then he must have been Abel and the other prince must have been Benjamin.
3. Therefore, both lied.

23. The Ogre's Boast: 100 or none.

	A	B	C	D	E	F	G	H
Ogre	T	T	T	T	F	F	F	F
Kay	T	T	F	F	T	T	F	F
Abel	T	F	F	T	T	F	T	F

1. We can eliminate A, B, D and E possibilities, because they indicate that *two* of the statements are true, and we are told that only one statement is true.
2. We can eliminate H, because it indicates that all the statements are false, and we know that one is true.

3. That leaves three possibilities: C, F and G.

	C	F	G
Ogre	T	F	F
Kay	F	T	F
Abel	F	F	T

4. If the ogre's claim that he devoured more than 100 is true, then Sir Kay's statement that the ogre ate *fewer* than 100 is false. But Abel's statement that the ogre ate at least one *can't* be false. So C is eliminated.
5. G need not be contradictory. Suppose the ogre's boast of more than 100 and Sir Kay's statement of less than 100 are false. Abel's statement that the ogre ate at least one could be true—if the ogre ate exactly 100.
6. As for F—if Sir Kay's statement that the ogre devoured fewer than 100 is true, then the ogre's claim is false. And Abel's statement that the ogre devoured at least one could also be false—if the ogre ate none!

24. Heads for Hats: Yes, they went free. Paula was wearing a white hat.

Princess Paula thought it through this way:
1. If both Benjamin and I are wearing red hats, Abel would know that he is wearing a white hat because there are only two red hats.
2. Benjamin knows from Abel's confusion that either he or I or both of us are wearing a white hat.
3. Benjamin sees the color of my hat, but he still doesn't know what color hat he is wearing.
4. If my hat is red, Benjamin would know his own hat is white.
5. Therefore, my hat is white.

No matter how many princes and princesses are captured, as long as the number of hats of one color is one less than the number of prisoners, at least one of them will always have a hat of the other color. Thus, the last one can always figure out the color of his or her own hat.

With three people involved, there are eight possible combinations:

	1	2	3	4	5	6	7	8
Abel	W	W	W	W	R	R	R	R
Benjamin	W	W	R	R	W	R	W	R
Paula	W	R	R	W	W	W	R	R
	X	X					X	X

1. Condition 8 is obviously impossible because there are only two red hats.
2. We can eliminate condition 3 when Abel can not tell the color of his hat. Since there were only two red hats, he would have known he had a white one if the other two wore red.
3. We can eliminate condition 7 because Benjamin could not tell the color of his hat. If the other two were wearing red, he would have known he was wearing white.
4. We can eliminate condition 2. If Paula's hat had been red, Benjamin would have known his own hat was white since both hats could not have been red.
5. In every other condition, Paula's hat is white.

25. Hidden Gold: The merchant divided the jars into groups of three and then set three jars aside. He placed three of the other six on each pan of the scale. The scale balanced, and so he knew that the jar with the gold was among three jars he had not weighed. He put aside the six jars he had already weighed.

Next he took two of the three jars not yet weighed and placed them on each pan of the scale. He knew that if they balanced, the third jar was the one that held the gold.

But they did not balance. Then which was the jar with the gold? Was it the one that was heavier or lighter?

He removed the lighter jar and put it aside. Then he replaced it on the scale with one of the six jars he had weighed initially and which he knew did not contain the gold. When the two jars still did not balance, he knew the heavier jar held the gold.

26. Baskets and Baskets: He balanced four of the baskets on each side of the scale. When they did not balance, he knew that the basket of pig food was among those on the heavier side of the scale.

If they had balanced, he would have known that the pig food was in the four that he did not weigh.

In either case, it took only one weighing for him to avoid the basket of pig fodder.

27. Wanted—Pig Food: It took two more weighings.

Dividing the heavier group of four baskets, he placed two on each side of the scale. The group of two that was heavier contained the pig fodder.

He put aside the two lighter baskets and divided the other two so that one was on each side of the scale. The one that was heavier this time was the pig fodder.

28. Lead Weight: With the 1, 2, 4, and 8 ounce weights, the merchant could weigh any object from one ounce to 15 ounces.

Using weights of 1, 2 and the successive powers of 2, he could weigh up to, but not including, twice the heaviest weight. With two weights, 1 and 2, he could weigh up to and including 3 ounces.

With the 4-ounce weight, he could weigh 4, 5 (4 + 1), 6 (4 + 2), and 7 (4 + 2 + 1).

With the 8-ounce weight, he could weigh 8, 9 (8 + 1), 10 (8 + 2), 11 (8 + 2 + 1), 12 (8 + 4), 13 (8 + 4 + 1), 14 (8 + 4 + 2), and 15 (8 + 4 + 2 + 1) ounces.

29. Heavier Stakes: 1, 3, 9, and 27 pounds.

To weigh an object of two pounds, the merchant would

add the 1-pound weight on the same side as the 2-pound object and balance it with the 3-pound weight on the other side: $2 = 3 - 1$.

To weigh a 4-pound object, he would balance the object with both the 1-pound and the 3-pound weight on the other side: $4 = 3 + 1$.

To weigh a 40-pound object, he would balance the object with all four weights on the other side: $40 = 1 + 3 + 9 + 27$.

30. Weighty Matters:

a) $9 - 3 - 1 = 5$ c) $27 = 27$

b) $27 - 9 - 3 - 1 = 14$ d) $27 - 3 + 1 = 25$

With the 9 pound weight, he could weigh objects from 5 pounds up to and including 13 pounds $(9 + 4)$. To weigh a 5-pound object, he would place the 3-pound weight and the 1-pound weight on the same side as the object and balance it with the 9-pound weight $(9 - 3 - 1)$. He used the same method for the 6-pound object $(9 - 3)$.

To weigh a 7-pound object, he would place the 3-pound weight with the object and the 9-pound weight and the 1-pound weight on the other side $(9 + 1 - 3)$. For an 8-pound object he would use $(9 - 1)$; 10 $(9 + 1)$; 11 $(9 + 3 - 1)$; 12 $(9 + 3)$; 13 $(9 + 3 + 1)$.

And with the 27-pound weight he could weigh from 14 to 40 pounds $(13 + 27)$. To weigh an object of 14 pounds, he would add to the object the 1, 3 and 9-pound weights while the 27-pound weight was on the other side: $(27 - 1 - 3 - 9)$.

For a 15-pound object: $(27 - 3 - 9)$; 16 $(27 - 3 - 9 + 1)$; 17 $(27 - 1 - 9)$; 18 $(27 - 9)$; 19 $(27 - 9 + 1)$; 20 $(27 - 9 - 1 + 3)$; 21 $(27 - 9 + 3)$; 22 $(27 - 9 + 3 + 1)$; 23 $(27 - 1 - 3)$; 24 $(27 - 3)$; 25 $(27 - 3 + 1)$; 26 $(27 - 1)$; 27 (27); 28 $(27 + 1)$; 29 $(27 - 1 + 3)$; 30 $(27 + 3)$; 31 $(27 + 3 + 1)$; 32 $(27 + 9 - 3 - 1)$; 33 $(27 + 9 - 3)$; 34 $(27 + 9 + 1 - 3)$; 35 $(27 + 9 - 1)$; 36 $(27 + 9)$; 37 $(27 + 9 + 1)$; 38 $(27 + 9 + 3 - 1)$; 39 $(27 + 9 + 3)$; 40 $(27 + 9 + 3 + 1)$.

31. Gold and Silver Coins: He took one coin from the first sack, two from the second, three from the third, and so on, until he had all ten from the tenth. Then he carefully stacked and weighed them.

In all he weighed 55 coins (1 + 2 + 3 + 4 + 5 + 6 + 7 + 8 + 9 + 10). Since each gold piece weighed ten grams, if all had been gold, the scale would have read 550 grams.

The amount by which the weight was too light indicated the number of silver coins and the number of the silver sack. For instance, if the weight was 543 grams, it would indicate that seven silver coins (550 − 543 = 7) had been weighed with the gold coins and that the rest of the silver coins were in the seventh sack.

32. The Brothers Four:

	Pig	Donkey	Camel	Goat
Ahmed	N			N
Sharif	N		N	
Abou	N			N
Omar			N	N

1. By filling in the boxes with the information from statements 1, 2, 4, and 5, we learn that Omar must have been a pig and Sharif a goat.

	Pig	Donkey	Camel	Goat
Ahmed	N			N
Sharif	N		N	Y
Abou	N			N
Omar	Y		N	N

2. Omar *was* a pig. Therefore, according to the conditional statement 3, Ahmed had to be a camel.

	Pig	Donkey	Camel	Goat
Ahmed	N	N	Y	N
Sharif	N	N	N	Y
Abou	N		N	N
Omar	Y	N	N	N

3. Abou was a donkey.

33. Beasts of Burden: Sharif, the goat, always carried oil.

	A	B	C	D	E	F	G	H
Donkey	o	o	o	o	d	d	d	d
Goat	o	o	d	d	o	o	d	d
Camel	o	d	o	d	o	d	o	d
	X		X	X			X	X

1. Condition 1 tells us that if the donkey carried dates, then the goat carried oil. This eliminates G and H.
2. Condition 2 tells us that if the donkey bore oil, then the camel carried dates. This eliminates A and C.
3. Condition 3 tells us that if the goat carried dates, then the camel carried oil. This eliminates D.
4. B has no conflict. It indicates that the donkey and the goat both carried oil, and the camel carried dates. This is consistent with Condition 2 which states that if the donkey carried oil, then the camel carried dates. Condition 1 tells us that if the donkey carried dates, then the goat carried oil. However, if the donkey did not carry dates, the goat could have carried either dates or oil. Condition 3 tells us that if the goat carried dates, then the camel carried oil. Since the goat did not carry dates, the camel could have carried either dates or oil.

5. E has no conflict. It indicates that the donkey carried dates, while the goat and the camel both carried oil. Condition 1 tells us that if the donkey carried dates, then the goat carried oil. Since the donkey did not carry oil, we can infer from condition 2 that the camel could have carried either dates or oil. Since the goat did not carry dates, we can infer from condition 3 that the camel could have carried either dates or oil.

6. F has no conflict. It indicates that the donkey and the camel carried dates, the goat carried oil. Condition 1 tells us that if the donkey carried dates, the goat carried oil. Since the donkey carried dates, not oil, we can infer from condition 2 that the camel could have carried either. Since the goat carried oil, not dates, we can similarly infer, from condition 3, that there is no conflict in the camel carrying dates.

7. The only one whose burden we can be sure of is the goat. In all three possible situations, B, E and F, the goat always carried oil.

	B	E	F
Donkey	o	d	d
Goat	o	o	o
Camel	d	o	d

34. Feed Bags: Abou always ate from the feed bag containing hay.

	A	B	C	D	E	F	G	H
Abou	O	O	O	O	H	H	H	H
Horse	O	O	H	H	O	O	H	H
Cow	O	H	O	H	O	H	O	H

1. Condition 1 indicates that if Abou ate oats, then the horse ate what the cow ate. This eliminates B and C.
2. Condition 2 indicates that if the horse ate oats, then Abou ate what the cow did not. This eliminates A and F.
3. Condition 3 indicates that if the cow ate hay, Abou ate what the horse ate. This eliminates D.
4. The only situations with no conflict are E, G and H.
5. In each of those situations Abou, and only Abou, ate the same thing. He ate from the feed bag holding hay.

	E	G	H
Abou	H	H	H
Horse	O	H	H
Cow	O	O	H

35. The First Magic Number: 75.

50	51	52	53	54	55	56	57	58	59
60	61	62	63	64	65	66	67	68	69
70	71	72	73	74	75	76	77	78	79

1. Condition A eliminates all multiples of 2 except those from 50 to 59. Eliminated therefore are 60, 62, 64, 66, 68 and 70, 72, 74, 76 and 78.

50	51	52	53	54	55	56	57	58	59
60	61	62	63	64	65	66	67	68	69
70	71	72	73	74	75	76	77	78	79

2. Condition B indicates that if the number was not a multiple of 3, it was a number from 60 through 69. This eliminates 50, 52, 53, 55, 56, 58, 59 and 71, 73, 77 and 79.

50	51	52	53	54	55	56	57	58	59
60	61	62	63	64	65	66	67	68	69
70	71	72	73	74	75	76	77	78	79

3. Condition C indicates that if the number was not a multiple of 4, then it was a number from 70 through 79. This eliminates 51, 54, 57 and 61, 63, 65, 67 and 69.

50	51	52	53	54	55	56	57	58	59
60	61	62	63	64	65	66	67	68	69
70	71	72	73	74	75	76	77	78	79

4. The remaining number, 75, satisfies all three conditions.
   A. It is not a multiple of 2 and so it does not have to be a number from 50 through 59.
   B. It is a multiple of 3, and so it does not have to be a number from 60 through 69.
   C. It is not a multiple of 4, and so it is, necessarily, a number from 70 through 79.

36. The Second Magic Number: 64.

37. The Third Magic Number: 44.

38. Seth Meets the Dragon:

	Pond	5-Cup Pitcher	3-Cup Pitcher	
1.	−5	5	0	Seth fills the 5-cup pitcher from the pond.
2.	−5	2	3	From the 5-cup pitcher, he fills the 3-cup pitcher, leaving two cups in the 5-cup pitcher.
3.	−3	2	0	He empties the 3-cup pitcher into the pond.
4.	−2	0	2	He pours the two cups of liquid from the 5-cup pitcher into the 3-cup pitcher.
5.	−7	5	2	Next he fills the 5-cup pitcher again.

	Pond	5-Cup Pitcher	3-Cup Pitcher	
6.	−7	4	3	From the full 5-cup pitcher, he fills the 3-cup pitcher. Since there are already two cups in the 3-cup pitcher, this takes one cup only, leaving four cups in the 5-cup pitcher.
7.	−4	4	0	He empties the 3-cup pitcher into the pond.

39. The Second Challenge:

	12-Cup Pitcher	7-Cup Pitcher	5-Cup Pitcher	
	12	0	0	Seth fills the 7-cup pitcher from the 12-cup pitcher, leaving five cups in the 12-cup pitcher.
1.	5	7	0	
2.	5	2	5	From the 7-cup pitcher he fills the 5-cup pitcher, leaving two cups in the 7-cup pitcher.
3.	10	2	0	He empties the 5-cup pitcher back into the 12-cup pitcher, which now has ten cups of water.
4.	10	0	2	He pours the two cups of water from the 7-cup pitcher into the 5-cup pitcher.
5.	3	7	2	He refills the 7-cup pitcher from the 12-cup pitcher, leaving three cups of water in the 12-cup pitcher.

	12-Cup Pitcher	7-Cup Pitcher	5-Cup Pitcher	
6.	3	4	5	From the 7-cup pitcher he fills the 5-cup pitcher, leaving four cups of water in the 7-cup pitcher.
7.	8	4	0	He empties the 5-cup pitcher back into the 12-cup pitcher, which now contains eight cups of water.
8.	8	0	4	He pours the four cups of water in the 7-cup pitcher into the 5-cup pitcher.
9.	1	7	4	He fills the 7-cup pitcher from the eight cups in the 12-cup pitcher, leaving one cup of water in the 12-cup pitcher.
10.	1	6	5	He fills the 5-cup pitcher with one cup from the 7-cup pitcher, leaving six cups of water in the 7-cup pitcher.
11.	6	6	0	He pours the five cups of water in the 5-cup pitcher back into the 12-cup pitcher. Both the 12- and the 7-cup pitcher now have six cups of water.

40. The Three Steps: By pouring the water from the largest jug into the smallest jug first, Seth measures out the four litres in three steps. If he had poured into the middle jug first, it would have taken five steps.

A.

	8-Litre Jug	3-Litre Jug	2-Litre Jug
	8	0	0
1.	6	0	2
2.	6	2	0
3.	4	2	2

B.

	8-Litre Jug	3-Litre Jug	2-Litre Jug
	8	0	0
1.	5	3	0
2.	5	1	2
3.	3	3	2
4.	6	0	2
5.	4	2	2

41. Wicked Walter: Seth pours first into the larger urn.

A.

	10-Gallon Urn	4-Gallon Urn	3-Gallon Urn
	10	0	0
1.	6	4	0
2.	6	1	3
3.	9	1	0
4.	9	0	1
5.	5	4	1

If he had poured first into the smaller empty urn, he would have needed twice as many steps.

B.

	10-Gallon Urn	4-Gallon Urn	3-Gallon Urn
	10	0	0
1.	7	0	3
2.	7	3	0
3.	4	3	3
4.	4	4	2
5.	6	4	0
7.	6	1	3
8.	9	1	0
9.	9	0	1
10.	5	4	1

42. Drop by Drop: Seth measures out the three drops in four steps, and four drops in six steps.

Filling the 5-drop vial first takes four steps to get three drops* and fourteen steps to get four drops.**

Filling the 7-drop vial first takes sixteen steps to get the three drops· but only six steps to get the four drops.··

A.	5-Drop Vial	7-Drop Vial	B.	7-Drop Vial	5-Drop Vial
1.	5	0		7	0
2.	0	5		2	5
3.	5	5		2	0
4.	*3	7		0	2
5.	3	0		7	2
6.	0	3		··4	5
7.	5	3		4	0
8.	1	7		0	4
9.	1	0		7	4
10.	0	1		6	5
11.	5	1		6	0
12.	0	6		1	5
13.	5	6		1	0
14.	**4	7		0	1
15.				7	1
16.				·3	5

43. Triple Threat: There are at least five ways to get three litres into three jars. Pouring into the 5-pint jar first, however, requires seven steps, while pouring into either of the smaller jars involves only six steps.

A.		9-Pint Jar	5-Pint Jar	4-Pint Jar	2-Pint Jar
		9	0	0	0
	1.	4	5	0	0
	2.	4	3	0	2
	3.	4	0	3	2
	4.	6	0	3	0
	5.	1	5	3	0
	6.	1	3	3	2
	7.	3	3	3	0

Pint Jars

B.	9-	5-	4-	2-		C.	9-	5-	4-	2-
	9	0	0	0			9	0	0	0
1.	5	0	4	0		1.	5	0	4	0
2.	5	4	0	0		2.	3	0	4	2
3.	1	4	4	0		3.	3	2	4	0
4.	1	5	3	0		4.	3	5	1	0
5.	1	3	3	2		5.	3	3	1	2
6.	3	3	3	0		6.	3	3	3	0

D.	9-	5-	4-	2-		E.	9-	5-	4-	2-
	9	0	0	0			9	0	0	0
1.	7	0	0	2		1.	7	0	0	2
2.	7	2	0	0		2.	3	0	4	2
3.	3	2	4	0		3.	3	2	4	0
4.	3	5	1	0		4.	3	5	1	0
5.	3	3	1	2		5.	3	3	1	2
6.	3	3	3	0		6.	3	3	3	0

44. The Rescue:

	Vat A	Vat B	5-Pint Pitcher	4-Pint Pitcher
	10 gallon	10 gallons	0	0
	80 pints	80 pints	0 pints	0 pints
1.	75	80	5	0
2.	75	80	1	4
3.	79	80	1	0
4.	79	80	0	1
5.	74	80	5	1
6.	74	80	2	4
7.	78	80	2	0
8.	78	76	2	4
9.	80	76	2	2

45. The Well of Wisdom: ½ or a 50% chance. A coin has two sides. When it falls, one side or the other—either the head or tail—will face upwards, with each side equally likely. The chance of the tossed coin showing heads is one of two possibilities.

We don't need help to derive the answer when there are only two possibilities. However, as the possibilities increase, we do, and we can devise a formula that will help us reason and provide a short cut.

Formula:
x = number of ways a favorable outcome can occur
y = number of ways an unfavorable outcome can occur
N = total number of possible events (x + y)
P = probability of success

Probability of favorable outcome:
$$P = x/x + y = x/N$$

46. Evelynne at the Well: ¼ or 25%. Here are the possibilities:

Merlin's Coin	Evelynne's Coin
heads	tails
tails	tails
tails	heads
heads	heads

The chance of two heads coming up is one of four possibilities. Again, we don't need the formula for finding the answer to such a simple problem, but let's take a look at how it works. It's easier to understand a formula, when you're not dependent on it for the solution.

The formula for joint occurrence:

$$P (a \text{ and } b) = P (a) \times P (b)$$
P = possibility of occurrence (success)

a = Merlin's chance of getting a head = ½
b = Evelynne's chance of getting a head = ½

P (a) × P (b) = ?
P (a) × P (b) = ½ × ½ = ¼

The probability of Merlin and Evelynne both pitching heads is one in four.

47. And Percival Makes Three: $\frac{1}{8}$ or $12\frac{1}{2}\%$.

There are eight possibilities:

Merlin	Evelynne	Percival
tails	tails	tails
tails	tails	heads
tails	heads	tails
tails	heads	heads
heads	tails	tails
heads	tails	heads
heads	heads	tails
heads	heads	heads

Each of the three players has one chance in two of tossing a head.

The formula: $\frac{1}{2} \times \frac{1}{2} \times \frac{1}{2} = \frac{1}{8}$

The chance is one in eight that all three coins will come up heads.

48. Four Coins in the Well: $\frac{1}{16}$ or $6\frac{1}{4}\%$.

For each coin it is one of two possibilities or $\frac{1}{2}$. Since there are four tosses, the formula: $\frac{1}{2} \times \frac{1}{2} \times \frac{1}{2} \times \frac{1}{2} = \frac{1}{16}$.

There is one chance in 16 that all four tosses will come up heads. If you list the possibilities, you'll see that:

Merlin	Evelynne	Percival	Vivienne
tails	tails	tails	tails
tails	tails	heads	tails
tails	heads	tails	tails
tails	heads	heads	tails
heads	tails	tails	tails
heads	tails	heads	tails
heads	heads	tails	tails
heads	heads	heads	tails
tails	tails	tails	heads
tails	tails	heads	heads
tails	heads	tails	heads
tails	heads	heads	heads
heads	tails	tails	heads
heads	tails	heads	heads
heads	heads	tails	heads
heads	heads	heads	heads

49. Oberon's Toss: ½ or 50%. Oberon's coin can come up in one of two ways, heads or tails. There is one chance in two that it will be tails.

50. How Many Wiser Wizards? 14. Half, or 14, of the apprentices can be expected to match the previously pitched coin. Each pitch has one chance in two of matching the previous pitch. Of course, there is always the *possibility*, though a slim one, that all will win.

51. Magic Seeds: ⅓.

Titania	Garth
black 1	white
black 2	white
white	black 1
white	black 2
black 1	black 2
black 2	black 1

Since there are two black seeds and one white seed, Titania's chances of getting a black one are two out of three or ⅔. If Titania draws a black seed, then there are just one black and one white left. Therefore, Garth's chances are one of two or ½. The odds that they both get black seeds: ⅔ × ½ = ²⁄₆ = ⅓.

52. Blind Sorcerer's Buff: ¹⁄₂₅₆. Since there are four corners, the formula is: ¼ × ¼ × ¼ × ¼ = ¹⁄₂₅₆.

53. Encore: ¹⁄₂₄. The first apprentice to start "home" has four corners to choose from, and so his chances are one in four of getting back to his original corner. The second apprentice has three chances of getting back to her original corner. The third has one in two chances, and the last, with only one corner remaining, one in one. The formula: ¼ × ⅓ × ½ × ¹⁄₁ = ¹⁄₂₄.

54. Non-Magic Magic: Urth. Since there are four aces in a deck of 52 cards, Lorelei's chances of coming up with an ace are $\frac{4}{52}$, or $\frac{1}{13}$ (one in thirteen chances). Since there are 13 hearts, Urth's possibility of coming up with a heart are $\frac{13}{52}$, or $\frac{1}{4}$ (one in four chances).

55. More Card Tricks: If Lorelei draws an ace the first time, she has a better chance of being a successful magician if she puts it back into the pack. If she puts the ace back, her chances of getting two aces are: $\frac{4}{52} \times \frac{4}{52} = \frac{1}{13} \times \frac{1}{13} = \frac{1}{169}$. If she puts the ace aside, her chances of getting two aces are: $\frac{4}{52} \times \frac{3}{51} = \frac{1}{13} \times \frac{1}{17} = \frac{1}{221}$.

56. Hearts for Urth: If Urth draws a heart the first time and puts it back in the deck, the probability of two hearts is: $\frac{13}{52} \times \frac{13}{52} = \frac{1}{4} \times \frac{1}{4} = \frac{1}{16}$. If he puts the first heart aside, the probability of two hearts is: $\frac{1}{4} \times \frac{12}{51} = \frac{12}{204} = \frac{1}{17}$.

57. Go Fish: Pendragon has a better chance of getting an enchanted fish if he goes first. Since there are thirty fish, two of which are enchanted, Pendragon has 2 possibilities in 30 of getting the special fish if he goes first: $\frac{2}{30} = \frac{1}{15}$. With nine fish eliminated (one with a gift), he has only one chance in 21 of getting an enchanted fish: $\frac{1}{21}$.

58. Two Enchanted Fish?: $\frac{1}{435}$. ($\frac{2}{30} \times \frac{1}{29} = \frac{2}{870} = \frac{1}{435}$).

59. Martian Locomotion: D. The Martian turns 45 degrees counterclockwise each time it moves.

60. The Dragon's Pitchers: B—the 4-ounce pitcher. Each pitcher holds half as many ounces as the one before it.

61. Merlin Waves a Wand: C. Each dragon and knight moves to the left.

62. Martian Manners: B. Feathered Martians who find themselves next to finned Martians turn their backs on them.

63. Knights and Their Weapons: C. Only the knight and the weapon next to one another move—the knight up, the weapon down.

64. The Missing Swords: C. Number and direction are involved. There are three sets of single swords, three sets of double swords, but only two sets of three swords. None of the swords points downwards.

65. The Genie and the Coins: A. Double the number of coins in the preceding box and add 1 (2 + 1 = 3, 6 + 1 = 7, 14 + 1 = 15, 30 + 1 = 31).

66. Genie Power: A. The genie changes the form of the creature next to him.

67. Genie Horseplay: B. The horse immediately to the left of the genie grows. The horse to the immediate right of the genie shrinks.

68. Martian Square Dance: D. In #2 the large Martians change places. In #3 the small Martians change places. In #4, the large and small spotted Martians change places. So in #5, the large and small striped Martians change places.

69. Genie Hijinks: C. The foods spin counterclockwise around animals.

70. Medieval Merry-Go-Round: D. Black and white knights and ladies alternate as they spin counterclockwise. Horse and dragon spin clockwise.

Index